THAI

Thai recipes for
the adventurous cook

THAI

THAI RECIPES FOR THE ADVENTUROUS COOK

Quantum
Books

A QUANTUM BOOK

Published by
Quantum Books Ltd
6 Blundell Street
London N7 9BH

1-86160-199-9

Project Manager: Rebecca Kingsley
Designer: Bruce Low
Editor: Sarah Harris

The material in this publication previously appeared in
Thai Cooking

QUMTHAI
Set in Fritz Quadrata
Reproduced in Singapore by Eray Scan
Printed in Singapore by Star Standard Industries (Pte) Ltd

Contents
····

INTRODUCTION

The popularity of Thai cuisine has grown enormously in the past few years. Thai restaurants are now commonplace throughout the West, and, as many of the ingredients have become more widely available, more and more people are creating exotic Thai dishes in their own homes. Many of the spices, pickles and  sauces used in Thai cookery are readily available in larger supermarkets, as well as in specialist shops.

Sharing similarities with other Eastern cuisines, in that most dishes are based around rice or noodles, the distinctive flavour of Thai food is often considered more delicate than its more mainstream counterparts. Thai recipes tend to favour fish and vegetables over meats, although poultry is also featured. Yet it is the combination of spices and chillies that characterises Thai food, and provides its distinctive flavour.

Positioned between India and China, Thailand has been able to draw upon the influences of its neighbours over the centuries; blending the different facets together to produce something unique. This is true in terms of all aspects of Thailand's culture - from politics and art, to cookery.

Yet it is not only Thailand's proximity to India and China that accounts for the vast diversity of dishes found in Thai cuisine. It is also situated on a major maritime route, so has also been exposed to a range of influences from further afield. Interestingly, as a cuisine noted for its use of chillies, these were not originally grown in Thailand, instead originating in South and Central America. That these have been assimilated so successfully into traditional Thai cookery is another example of Thailand's skill in blending influences from other cultures.

Although not yet as familiar in the West, Thai cooking also offers regional diversity. A dish served near the Chinese border, for example, will differ considerably from one served on the opposite side of the country. As the regional specialities of China and India are now familiar across the world, it can only be a matter of time before the distinctions between the regional cuisines of Thailand become equally well known.

Although, inevitably, Thai cooking has been influenced by Western cooking techniques, most Thai recipes still utilise traditional methods. Most dishes are steamed, boiled or fried, and food is generally cooked on the top of the stove, rather than in an oven.

Stir-frying is another influence readily adopted from China, and is a particularly popular cooking technique. The rapid cooking of ingredients preserves much of their natural goodness, and also avoids too much absorption of fat - both ideal in today's health-conscious society. When stir-frying, it is important to keep the heat high, as food cooked too slowly can easily go limp and tasteless. Ingredients, particularly hard vegetables, should be cut into bite-sized chunks, to allow everything to cook completely.

Steaming is another healthy cooking method, as much the natural goodness of the food is retained. Fish is frequently steamed, often wrapped in banana leaves which add a subtle flavour. Vegetables also benefit from steaming. It is important not to overfill the saucepan when steaming food, to avoid sogginess, but equally important not to let your pan boil dry.

The basic cooking utensils you will need to produce tasty Thai meals are a wok, a deep saucepan and a steamer. Special Chinese steamer sets made from either aluminium or bamboo are readily available, although a metal colander covered with a lid is just as effective. A wooden spoon or spatula for stir frying and a slotted spoon or wire mesh scoop are also useful.

Unlike Western meals, which generally include one dish per course, a Thai menu traditionally includes a variety of dishes, often served together. Each guest helps themselves from the main dishes, which are usually accompanied by rice or noodles. Less importance is placed on the order of eating, as dishes are chosen to complement each other, providing a healthy and delicious balance of ingredients and flavours.

Preparation is particularly important in Thai cookery. Many of the dishes are cooked quickly, so ingredients should be easily to hand when needed. Most of the preparation involves peeling and chopping, and as most dishes have quite a lot of ingredients, it is better to have two chopping boards if possible. Although most spices today are available dried or powdered, many people find that recipes are enhanced by using fresh herbs and spices whenever possible. If this is your preference, a mortar and pestle are useful tools.

Most of the ingredients, such as fish and vegetables can be bought anywhere. Some of the special ingredients may require a trip into a larger supermarket, or specialist store. These include pickled

garlic, dried chillies, dried fish and fish sauce. It is a good idea to check through the recipes, and buy all your special requirements in one shopping trip.

The recipes in this book have been chosen to allow the adventurous cook to experiment with a wide variety of ingredients, cooking methods and flavours. With a wealth of ingredients to draw upon, Thai cooking offers delicious recipes to suit every palate - from mild to fiery. So with preparation, a little time and a lot of enjoyment, you can create a range of healthy and delicious menus for friends and family.

CHAPTER ONE

BEEF AND PORK

NORTH-EASTERN SAUSAGES

Sai Krok Issaan

SERVES 4 – 6

INGREDIENTS

100 g (4 oz) ground pork

50 g (2 oz) cooked rice

2 tbsp lime juice

1 tsp chopped garlic

1 tsp ground white pepper

½ tsp salt

¼ tsp sugar

50 cm sausage casing, rubbed with salt and rinsed

600 ml (1pt) peanut or corn oil for frying

Take the pork, rice, lime juice, garlic, pepper, salt and sugar, and mix well. Stuff into the sausage casing, and tie along the length with string into small balls. Chill in the refrigerator for 24 hours.

Prick the sausage with a cocktail stick. Heat the oil to 180°C /350°F / gas 4 in a pan and fry the sausage on both sides until brown and well cooked, about 15 minutes. Cut into individual sausages.

Serve accompanied by fresh sliced ginger, fresh cabbage, fresh small green chillies, peanuts, spring onions and coriander leaves.

COCONUT BEEF CURRY
Panaeng Neua

SERVES 8

INGREDIENTS

75 ml (2½ floz) peanut or corn oil

300 g (11 oz) beef sirloin, cut into 3 × 2 × ½ cm pieces

900 ml (3 floz) thin coconut milk

1 tbsp fish sauce (available in bottles)

2 tsp sugar

2 fresh red chillies sliced

2 kaffir lime leaves, sliced finely

25 g (1 oz) sweet basil leaves

Curry Paste

6 dried red chillies, chopped roughly

7 white peppercorns

35 g (1½ oz) garlic, chopped roughly

25 g (1 oz) shallots, chopped roughly

2 coriander roots, chopped roughly

2 tsp salt

1 tsp roughly chopped galangal (ka)

1 tsp roughly chopped lemon grass

1 tsp roughly chopped kaffir lime zest

1 tsp shrimp paste

Pound all the curry paste ingredients together with a mortar and pestle or in a blender to form a paste.

Heat the oil in a pan or wok and fry the curry paste for 3–4 minutes. Add the beef and fry for 2 minutes, then add the coconut milk and boil until the beef is tender, about 15 minutes. Add the fish sauce, sugar and chilli. Remove from the heat, transfer to a serving plate and sprinkle with the lime zest and basil.

Serve accompanied by rice.

NORTHERN PORK CURRY
Kaeng Hang Lei

SERVES 6

INGREDIENTS

4 stalks lemon grass, chopped

I tbsp chopped galangal (ka)

I tbsp shrimp paste

4 dried red chillies, chopped

I kg (2¼ lb) pork belly, cut into small

I½ cm thick strips

900 ml (30 floz)cold waster

I tbsp turmeric

I tsp black soy sauce

I0 shallots, sliced

50 g (2oz) palm sugar

50 g (2oz) chopped and pounded ginger

75 ml (2½ floz) tamarind juice

2 tbsp chopped garlic

½ tbsp marinated soya beans

Fish sauce, to taste (optional)

Pound the lemon grass, galangal, shrimp paste and chillies with a mortar and pestle or in a blender until fine, then mix with the pork. Put in a pan with the water, turmeric and soy sauce. Bring to a boil and cook until tender, about 15 minutes, then add the rest of the ingredients. Boil again for 5–8 minutes and remove from the heat. Taste and season with fish sauce if necessary.

FRIED FLAT BEANS WITH PORK
Phad Sator

SERVES 4

3 fresh yellow or green chillies, chopped

1 tbsp chopped garlic

½ tsp shrimp paste

2 tbsp peanut or corn oil

125 g (5 oz) pork loin (or chicken, or shrimp), cut into thin strips

200 g (8 oz) fresh sator or lima beans

½ tsp fish sauce

½ tsp sugar

½ tsp lime or lemon juice

Pound the chillies and garlic together with a pestle and mortar or in a blender to a fine paste. Mix with the shrimp paste.

Heat the oil in a pan or wok. Add the chilli-garlic mixture, then add the pork and stir-fry for 3 minutes. Add the beans and all the remaining ingredients, plus 3 tbsp water if using lima beans, then fry until the beans are cooked, about 10 minutes – they should be quite firm.

Serve accompanied by rice.

Chapter Two

Fish and Seafood

Stuffed Squid Soup

■

Baby Clams with Chilli and Basil

■

Spicy Seafood salad

■

Fried Fish topped with Chilli Sauce

■

Steamed Fish Curry

■

Casseroled Prawns with Glass Noodles

■

Fried Catfish Spicy Salad

■

Green Chilli dip

■

Fried Fish with Pork and Ginger

■

Prawns with Lemon and Coconut

■

Stuffed Crab Shells

STUFFED SQUID SOUP
Kaeng Cheud Plaa Muk
SERVES 4

INGREDIENTS

100 g (4 oz) ground pork

½ tsp white soy sauce

¼ tsp ground white pepper

300 g (11 oz) squid, body not tentacles, cleaned

1200 ml (2 pt) chicken stock

½ tbsp preserved cabbage, chopped roughly

7 white peppercorns, crushed

5 garlic cloves, crushed

1 tsp fish sauce

¼ tsp sugar

3 spring onions, cut into 1½ cm pieces

2 tbsp coriander leaves and stems cut in ½ inch pieces

Mix the pork, soy sauce and white pepper together well and use to stuff the squid. If there is any extra pork mixture, form it into small meatballs.

Heat the chicken stock in a pan or wok, add the preserved cabbage, crushed peppercorns and garlic, and bring to a boil. Place the stuffed squid in the boiling stock, with meatballs if there are any, and then add the fish sauce and sugar. Boil until the stuffed squid is cooked, about 15 minutes or until it is no longer pink when cut into. Add the spring onion and coriander and remove from the heat immediately.

Serve accompanied by rice.

BABY CLAMS WITH CHILLI AND BASIL

Hoi Lai Phad Phrik Pao

SERVES 4

INGREDIENTS

Approx. 100 ml (3 floz) peanut or corn oil for frying

575 g (1 lb 6 oz) fresh baby clams in their shells, cleaned well

1½ tbsp chopped garlic

5 fresh red chillies, sliced lengthwise

2 tbsp red chilli paste

2 tsp white soy sauce

150 ml (5 floz) chicken stock

100 g (4oz) sweet basil leaves

Heat the oil in a pan or wok until quite hot, about 190°C/375°F/gas 5. Add the clams and garlic, and cook until the clams open slightly, 2–3 minutes. Add the fresh chillies, chilli paste, and soya sauce, mix well, then pour in the chicken stock. Bring to a boil, cook for 2 minutes, stir in the basil and serve immediately.

SPICY SEAFOOD SALAD
Yam Thalae
SERVES 6

Cook the fish, prawns and squid separately in salted water until cooked, about 2–3 minutes each, and drain.

Pound the chillies, garlic, coriander root, fish sauce and sugar together with a pestle and mortar or in a blender until fine. Place in a bowl and mix in the lemon juice, spring onions, onion and celery. Stir in the fish and seafood and mix well. Serve immediately.

INGREDIENTS

125 g (5 oz) sea bass or perch, cleaned, gutted and sliced thinly into strips
125 g (5 oz) large shrimp, shelled
125 g (5 oz) squid, body and tentacles, cleaned, gutted and slice into 2 cm strips
7 fresh small green chillies
5 garlic cloves
2 coriander roots
2 tbsp fish sauce
½ tsp sugar
2 tbsp lime or lemon juice
4 spring onions, sliced into ½ cm pieces
100 g (4 oz) onions, sliced thinly
50 g (2 oz) celery leaves and stems, sliced

FRIED FISH TOPPED WITH CHILLI SAUCE

Plaa Raad Phrik

SERVES 4 – 6

INGREDIENTS

8 garlic cloves

5 fresh yellow chiles

1 kg (2¼ lb) whole perch or sea bass, cleaned and gutted

Approx. 900 ml (30 floz) peanut or corn oil for frying

½ tsp each salt and ground white pepper

Plain flour for dusting

150 ml (5 floz) chicken stock

2 fresh red chilles, quartered lengthwise

1 tbsp tamarind juice or vinegar

2 tsp sugar

1 tsp fish sauce

25 g (10 oz) sweet basil leaves, fried in oil for 1 minute until crisp

Pound the garlic and chilli together lightly with a mortar and pestle or in a blender.

Score the fish on both sides 5–6 times, sprinkle on the salt and pepper and dust with flour. Heat the oil to 180°C/350°F /gas 4in a pan or wok and fry fish well, until crisp but tender inside, about 7–10 minutes. Remove and drain the fish and put in a serving dish.

Take out all except approx. 75 ml (2½ floz) of the oil. Then, cook the garlic and chile mixture, add the rest of the ingredients (except for the basil) and boil lightly for about 5 minutes until slightly thick. Pour on top of the fish and sprinkle over the fried basil to garnish.

STEAMED FISH CURRY
Haw Mok Plaa
SERVES 6 – 8

INGREDIENTS

300 g (11 oz) fish fillets (flounder, sole or seabass), skinned and cut into slices

750 ml (25 floz) thin coconut milk

2 eggs, beaten

3 tbsp fish sauce

100 g (4 oz) sweet basil leaves

100 g (4 oz) finely sliced cabbage

6 squares of banana leaf (optional)

1½ tbsp cornflour

2 kaffir lime leaves, torn into small pieces

1 fresh red chilli, seeded and cut into strips

Red Curry Paste

10 small garlic cloves, chopped lightly

5 dried red chillies, chopped lightly

5 white peppercorns

3 shallots, chopped lightly

2 coriander roots, sliced

1 tsp sliced galangal (ka)

1 tsp chopped lemon grass

½ tsp finely chopped kaffir lime zest

½ tsp salt

Pound all the ingredients for the paste together with a mortar and pestle or in a blender until fine. Put in a bowl and stir in the fish pieces, and 600 ml (20 floz) of the coconut milk. Break in the eggs and mix well. Stir in the fish sauce.

Divide the basil and cabbage between the banana leaf squares or 6–8 ovenproof ramekins or cups. Top with the fish mixture and wrap up. Cook in a pressure cooker, or bake in a 180°C/350°F/gas 4 oven, covered in a pan half-filled with hot water, for 10 minutes.

Meanwhile, boil the remaining 150 ml (5 floz) of coconut milk in a pan, and add the cornstarch to thicken slightly.

After the fish mixture has cooked for 10 minutes, spoon the thickened coconut milk over the tops and sprinkle with the lime leaf and chilli. Pressure-cook or bake again for 5 more minutes. Stand for 5 minutes before serving.

Serve accompanied by rice.

CASSEROLED SHRIMP WITH GLASS NOODLES

Kung Op Woon Sen

SERVES 6

Place all the soup stock ingredients in a pan, bring to a boil and simmer for 5 minutes. Leave to cool.

Take a heatproof casserole dish or heavy-bottomed pan and place the bacon over the base. Put in the prawns, coriander root, ginger, garlic and peppercorns. Place the noodles over the top, then add the butter, soy sauce and soup stock.

Place on the heat, cover, bring to a boil and simmer for 5 minutes. Mix well with tongs, add the coriander, cover and cook again until the shrimp are cooked, about 5 minutes more. Remove excess stock liquid before serving.

INGREDIENTS

2 bacon rashers, cut into 2.5 cm pieces
6 large prawns, shelled
2 coriander roots, cut in half
25 g (1 oz) ginger, pounded or chopped finely
25 g (1 oz)1 oz garlic, chopped
1 tbsp white peppercorns, crushed
500 g (20 oz) cellophane noodles (woon sen), soaked in cold water for 10 minutes
1 tsp butter
3 tbsp black soy sauce
50 g (1 oz) roughly chopped coriander leaves and stems

Soup Stock

600 ml (20 floz) chicken stock
2 tbsp oyster sauce
2 tbsp black soy sauce
½ tbsp sesame seed oil
1 tsp brandy or whisky
½ tsp sugar

FRIED CATFISH SPICY SALAD
Yam Plaa Duk Foo
SERVES 4 – 6

INGREDIENTS

2 whole catfish 475 g (1 lb 2 oz each),
cleaned and gutted

Approx. 1½ l (2½ pt) peanut or corn oil
for deep-frying

1 green unripe mango, cut into matchsticks

25 g (1 oz) unsalted roasted peanuts

7 fresh small green chillies, chopped

3 tbsp sliced shallots

3 tbsp fish sauce

2 tbsp coriander leaves and stems cut into
2½ cm pieces

Steam the catfish for 15 minutes until well cooked. Remove all the skin and bones and chop finely.

Heat the oil in a wok or pan until hot, about 108°C/350°F/ gas 4, sprinkle in the chopped fish and fry until light brown and crispy, 3–5 minutes. Remove with a slotted spoon or strainer and drain well.

Mix all the remaining ingredients except the coriander with the fish. Place the salad on plates, and garnish with coriander.

Serve accompanied by rice.

GREEN CHILLI DIP
Nam Phrik Num
SERVES 6

INGREDIENTS

1 tbsp chopped dried salted mackerel or anchovy

4 tbsp peanut or corn oil

10 fresh 5 cm green chillies, chopped roughly

10 garlic cloves, chopped roughly

6 shallots, chopped roughly

3 cherry tomatoes

2 tbsp hot water

1 tbsp chopped spring onion

1 tbsp chopped coriander leaves

Fish sauce, to taste (optional)

Fry the dried fish in the oil over medium heat for about 7–10 minutes and drain. Dry-fry the chillies, garlic, shallots and tomatoes until fragrant, about 8–10 minutes. Place in a bowl. Pound them lightly with the dry fish. Add the water, spring onion and coriander, and mix well. Taste to check: it should be of a sauce consistency and a touch salty; if not, add more water or fish sauce as required.

Serve accompanied by raw cabbage wedges, sliced cucumbers, raw string beans and/or fried or roasted fish.

INGREDIENTS

300 g (11 oz) whole pomfret fish, cleaned and gutted

½ tsp salt

50 g (2 oz) finely sliced pork belly or fresh fat back

2 salted preserved plums or 1 tbsp pickled lemon juice

60 g (3 oz) sliced ginger

10 small garlic cloves, crushed

25 g (1 oz) celery with its leaves, cut into 2.5 cm pieces

4 spring onions, cut into 1 inch pieces

2 fresh red chillies, cut into lengthwise strips

FRIED FISH WITH PORK AND GINGER

Plaa Jian

SERVES 4

Wash and dry the fish and rub it inside and out with the salt. Place half the pork fat on a heatproof plate that fits a steamer, put the fish on top and cover with the rest of the pork fat. Roughly chop the salted plum and sprinkle it (or the juice) over the top together with the ginger and garlic.

Steam for 15 minutes, then add the celery, spring onion and chilli and steam for 5 more minutes, until the fish is firm but tender.

Serve accompanied by rice.

PRAWNS WITH LEMON AND COCONUT

Kung Som

SERVES 4 – 6

INGREDIENTS

500 g (1 lb 2) oz raw large
prawns, shelled
300 ml (10 floz) thin coconut milk
2 tbsp lemon juice
¼ tsp fish sauce
¼ tsp sugar
¼ tsp salt
2 tbsp sliced shallots
5 fresh small green chillies, sliced into thin
circles

To butterfly the prawns, cut them lengthwise almost all the way through and splay them out.

Boil the coconut milk in a pan, add the prawns, cook for 1 minute and remove the pan from the heat. Allow to stand for about 1 minute (until the prawns are just cooked), then remove them with a slotted spoon and place on a serving plate.

Add the lemon juice, fish sauce, sugar and salt to the coconut milk in the pan, stir well for 1 minute and then spoon this sauce over the prawns. Sprinkle over the shallot and chilli.

Serve accompanied by rice.

STUFFED CRAB SHELLS

Poo Jaa

SERVES 4

4 blue crab shells, cleaned well

3 eggs, beaten well

Approx. 1½ l (2½ pt) peanut or corn oil for deep-frying

25 g (1 oz) coriander leaves

2 fresh red chillies, cut into lengthwise strips

Stuffing

50 g (2 oz) cooked ground pork

25 g (1 oz) ground shrimp

15 g (¾ oz) crab meat, fresh or drained very well if canned

2 tbsp finely chopped onion

1 tbsp finely sliced spring onion

1 tsp ground white pepper

1 tsp sugar

¼ tsp white soy sauce

¼ tsp salt

Mix all the stuffing ingredients together and fill the crab shells. Heat the oil in a pan or wok to approx. 180°C/350°F/gas 4.

Dip the stuffed crabs in the beaten egg to coat them well all over and then deep-fry until thoroughly cooked, about 10–15 minutes. Remove and drain well on kitchen paper. Sprinkle with the coriander and chilli before serving. Serve as an hors d'oeuvre or with rice and bottled Chinese plum sauce.

Chapter Three

Chicken and Duck

Fried Noodles with Chicken,
Vegetables and Gravy

■

Red Chicken Curry

■

Sweet and Sour Chicken

■

Chicken Fried with Cashew Nuts

■

Duck with Rice

■

Chicken Rice

■

Red Duck Curry

■

Chicken Fried with Basil

■

Chicken Fried Rice with Green Pepper

FRIED NOODLES WITH CHICKEN, VEGETABLES AND GRAVY

Kwitiaow Rad Naa

SERVES 4

INGREDIENTS

300 g (11 oz) large flat rice noodles

150 ml (5 floz) peanut or corn oil

1 tsp black soy sauce

2 tbsp garlic, chopped finely

200 g (7 oz) boneless skinned chicken breasts cut lengthwise into 1¾ cm thick slices

2 tbsp white soy sauce

2 tbsp sugar

1 tsp ground white pepper

1.8 l (3 pt) chicken stock

400 g (15 oz) kale or broccoli, cut into ½ inch pieces

1 tbsp cornflour, mixed with a little water

Boil the noodles for 1 minute and drain well. Heat half the oil in a wok or pan, add the noodles and fry lightly for 1 minute. Add the black soy sauce, fry lightly for another minute. Drain off the oil and transfer the noodles to a plate.

Heat the rest of the oil in the wok. Add the garlic and chicken, and fry lightly for 2 minutes. Stir in the white soy sauce, sugar, white pepper and then the chicken stock. Boil well for 3–5 minutes, add the kale, boil again for 1 minute and then add the cornflour. Boil for 1 minute and pour over the noodles.

Serve accompanied by sliced fresh red chilli in vinegar (phrik dong), fish sauce, sugar and chilli powder, in separate bowls.

RED CHICKEN CURRY

Kaeng Kai

SERVES 6

INGREDIENTS

1½ l (3 pt) thin coconut milk

1 quantity chilli paste

10 white peppercorns, crushed

300 g (11 oz) boneless skinned chicken breasts, cut across into ½ cm thick slices

3 tbsp fish sauce

½ tbsp palm sugar

7 small white aubergines, quartered

3 fresh red chillies, quartered lengthwise

2 kaffir lime leaves, torn into small pieces

25 g (1 oz) cup sweet basil leaves

Heat 300ml (½ pt) of the coconut milk in a pan, stir in the chili paste and white peppercorns, and cook for 2 minutes. Add the chicken slices, mix well and add the rest of the coconut milk. Bring to a boil, then add the fish sauce and palm sugar. Boil for 1 minute and then add the aubergine, chilli and lime leaf.

Bring back to a boil, cook for 3 minutes, add the basil, remove from the heat and serve.

SWEET AND SOUR CHICKEN

Priaw Waan Kai

SERVES 4 – 6

Heat the oil in a wok or pan, coat the chicken lightly with flour and fry it until light brown, about 5 minutes. Remove and drain on kitchen paper.

Remove all the oil except for about 100 ml (3 floz). Add the onion and pepper, cook for 1 minute, mix in the ketchup, and then add the remaining ingredients. Stir-fry for 1 minute, add the chicken and continue to cook until the onion is tender, about 2 minutes.

INGREDIENTS

1200 ml (2 pt) peanut or corn oil

400 g (15 oz) boneless skinned chicken breasts, cut across into ½ cm slices

Plain flour for coating

1 medium-sized onion, sliced

1 medium-sized green pepper, sliced

25 g (1 oz) tomato ketchup

25 g (1 oz) tomato quarters

25 g (1 oz) diced pineapple

150 ml (5 floz) chicken stock

2 tsp white soya sauce

1 tsp sugar

1 tsp white vinegar

CHICKEN FRIED WITH CASHEW NUTS

Kai Phad Met Ma Muang

SERVES 4

INGREDIENTS

300 g (11 oz) boneless skinned chicken
breasts, cut into slices

Plain flour for coating

300 ml (10 floz) peanut or corn oil

4 dried red chillies, fried and cut into 1½
cm pieces

1 tbsp chopped garlic

10 spring onions, white parts, cut into 5 cm
pieces

30 g (1½ oz) unsalted roasted cashew nuts

75 g (3 oz) onion, sliced

2 tbsp oyster sauce

1 tbsp white soy sauce

1 tbsp sugar

⅛ tsp black soy sauce

Coat the chicken lightly with flour. Heat the oil in a pan or wok and fry the chicken for about 5 minutes until light brown. Remove almost all the oil from the pan.

Add the chilli and garlic to the chicken in the pan and fry for 1 minute.

Add all the remaining ingredients; fry until cooked, about 3 more minutes.

DUCK WITH RICE
Khao Naa Ped

SERVES 4

Heat the ingredients for the cooked sauce together in a pan and boil for 1 minute. Mix the ingredients for the raw sauce in a bowl and put to one side.

Warm the duck and rice in a 180°C/ 350°F/ gas 4 oven for 5 minutes. Then, divide the rice between 4 serving plates, and arrange the duck meat over the top. Spoon the cooked sauce on top of each, and place ginger and pickle slices around the edges. Serve with the raw sauce on the side.

INGREDIENTS

1 roasted duck (rub with red food colouring before roasting), boned and cut into 6 x 1½ cm slices
500 g (2 lb) cooked rice
4 tbsp thinly sliced pickled ginger
4 tbsp thinly sliced sweet dill or pickled cucumber

Cooked Sauce

600 ml (1 pt) chicken stock
1 tbsp sugar
½ tbsp white soy sauce
¼ tbsp black soy sauce
1 tsp flour

Soya Chilli Rice

150 ml (5 floz) black soya sauce
3 fresh red chillies, sliced thinly into circles
1 tbsp sugar
½ tbsp vinegar

INGREDIENTS

300 g (11 oz) boneless skinned capon or
chicken breasts
1½ l (2½ pt) water
3 coriander roots
2 tsp salt
200 g (8 oz) rice, rinsed
10 garlic cloves, chopped
12 g (½ oz) ginger, sliced and crushed
3 tbsp peanut or corn oil
12½ cm piece of cucumber, cut into ½ cm
slices
25 g (1 oz) coriander leaves

Khao Man Sauce

5 fresh small green chiles, chopped
2 tbsp pickled soya beans
½ tbsp chopped ginger
½ tbsp white vinegar
1 tsp sugar
1 tsp black soya sauce
¼ tsp chopped garlic

CHICKEN RICE
Khao Man Kai
SERVES 4

Boil the water in a pan, add the chicken with the coriander root and salt, and cook until the chicken is soft, about 15 minutes. Remove the meat with a slotted spoon and put to one side. Strain the cooking liquid, put 1200 ml (2 pt) back in the pan and add the rice, garlic, ginger and oil. Bring back to a boil and cook, covered, until the rice is tender but not soft, about 15–18 minutes.

Place the rice on serving plates. Slice the chicken across into 1 cm pieces and place on top of the hot rice. Arrange the cucumber slices around the sides and sprinkle with the coriander leaves.

Mix all the ingredients for the caw mon sauce together in a bowl and serve with the chicken and rice, and with the remaining chicken broth if desired.

RED DUCK CURRY
Kaeng Ped Ped Yang
SERVES 6

Pound all the curry paste ingredients together with a mortar and pestle or in a blender to a fine paste.

Heat 600 ml (1 pt) of the coconut milk in a wok or pan, add the chilli paste mixture and cook together for 5 minutes. Add the rest of the coconut milk, bring to a boil, then add the duck, cherry tomatoes and red chilli. Bring back to the boil and then add the rest of the ingredients. Boil all together for 5 minutes and remove from the heat.

Serve accompanied by rice, salted eggs and sun-dried beef.

INGREDIENTS

2100 ml (3½ pt) thin coconut milk
1 roasted duck, boned with skin left on, cut into 1 cm slices
15 cherry tomatoes
5 fresh large red chillies, sliced lengthwise
50 g (2 oz) sweet basil leaves
3 kaffir lime leaves, chopped
3 tbsp sugar
2 tbsp fish sauce
1 tsp salt

Red Curry paste
3 stalks of lemon grass, sliced thinly
12 g (½ oz) chopped galangal (ka)
7 dried red chillies, chopped roughly
3 tbsp chopped garlic
1 tbsp shrimp paste
1 tsp chopped kaffir lime leaf
1 tsp chopped coriander root
1 tsp white peppercorns
½ tsp coriander seeds

43

CHICKEN FRIED WITH BASIL

Kai Phad Kaphrao

SERVES 4

Pound the green chilli and garlic together with a mortar and pestle or in a blender. Heat the oil in a wok or pan until hot, then add the chilli-garlic mixture. Fry for 1 minute. Add the chicken and stir-fry for 1 minute; then add the red chilli, oyster sauce, fish sauce and soy sauce. Stir-fry for 2 minutes, mix the basil in well and serve immediately.

Serve accompanied by rice.

INGREDIENTS

8 fresh green chillies, chopped lightly

8 garlic cloves, chopped lightly

75 ml (2½ floz) peanut or corn oil

300 g (11 oz) boneless skinned ground chicken

2 fresh red chiles, quartered lengthwise

1 tbsp oyster sauce

½ tsp fish sauce

¼ tsp black soya sauce

25 g (1 oz) sweet basil leaves

CHICKEN FRIED WITH GREEN PEPPER

Kai Phad Phrik

SERVES 4

Heat the oil in a wok or pan, add the garlic and chicken and fry well for a minute. Add the green pepper and chilli, mix, then add the onion and cook for 1 minute. One by one stir in the rest of the ingredients, cooking for about 30 seconds after each addition. Remove from the heat immediately after stirring in the basil.

Serve accompanied by rice.

INGREDIENTS

75 ml (2½ oz) peanut or corn oil

1 tbsp chopped garlic

300 g (11 oz) boneless skinned chicken breasts, cut lengthwise into 1cm thick slices

50 g (2 oz) sliced green pepper

5 fresh red chillies, sliced lengthwise

25 g (1 oz) thickly sliced onion

1 tbsp oyster sauce

½ tbsp white soy sauce

1 tsp fish sauce

¼ tsp black soy sauce

25 g (1 oz) sweet basil leaves

Chapter Four

Vegetables and Fruits

Pineapple Rice

∎

Green Mango Salad

∎

Green Papaya Salad

∎

Mixed Stir-Fried Vegetables

∎

Roasted Aubergine Salad

∎

Sticky Rice with Mangoes

∎

Stir-Fried Greens

∎

Thai-Fried Noodles

∎

Banana Cooked in Coconut Milk

∎

Fried Bananas

PINEAPPLE RICE
Khao op Sapparod
SERVES 4 – 6

Cut one side off the pineapple lengthwise to expose the inside. Carefully remove the inside fruit and cut into small dice. Reserve the outside of the pineapple.

Heat the oil in a pan or wok, add the ham and garlic, stir-fry, then add 25 g (1 oz) of the diced pineapple and all the rest of the ingredients. Mix well. Spoon into the empty pineapple, cover with the pineapple lid and bake in a preheated 140°C/275°F/gas 1 oven for 30 minutes.

INGREDIENTS

·1 pineapple
4 tbsp peanut or corn oil
600 g (24 oz) cooked rice
50 g (2 oz) finely diced ham
½ tbsp chopped garlic
30 g (1½ oz) raisins
2 tbsp chicken stock
2 tsp curry powder
1 tsp sugar
1 tsp salt
¼ tsp ground white pepper

GREEN MANGO SALAD
Yam Ma Muang
SERVES 4

INGREDIENTS

100 g (4 oz) green unripe mango flesh, cut into long matchsticks

50 g (2 oz) unsweetened grated coconut, dry-fried until light brown

25 g (1 oz) dried shrimp

3 tbsp sliced shallots

5 fresh small green chillies, chopped

1 tbsp palm sugar, or to taste

Fish sauce, to taste (optional)

Lime juice, to taste (optional)

Mix all the ingredients together. If not salty enough, add a little fish sauce; if not sour enough, add lime juice.

GREEN PAPAYA SALAD
Som Tam Thai

SERVES 4

INGREDIENTS

300 g (11 oz) green papaya, peeled and cut into long matchsticks

7 fresh small whole green chillies

6 garlic cloves, chopped roughly

50 g (2 oz) green string beans cut into 2.5 cm pieces

25 g (1oz) unsalted roasted peanuts

50 g (2 oz) dried small shrimp

6 cherry tomatoes, quartered

75 ml (2½ oz) lime or lemon juice

1 tbsp palm sugar

1 tbsp fish sauce

Take a little of the papaya, the chilli and garlic, and pound together lightly with a mortar and pestle or in a blender. Put in a bowl and stir in the beans, peanuts, prawns, tomato and the rest of the papaya. Mix well, then stir in the lemon juice, sugar and fish sauce.

Serve accompanied by raw vegetables chopped into bite-sized pieces—perhaps swamp cabbage and string beans—sticky rice and roasted chicken.

MIXED STIR-FRIED VEGETABLES

Phak Phad- Ruam Mit

SERVES 4

Mix all the ingredients together in a bowl, pour over the stock and add the white pepper.

Heat a wok or pan until lightly smoking and add the oil. When hot, add the garlic and stir well. Add the vegetables and liquid all at once (watch for splashing), and stir-fry until almost cooked, about 3–4 minutes; the vegetables should still be slightly crisp.

Add the oyster sauce and soy sauces, mix well for 1 minute and serve.

Serve accompanied by rice; this dish goes well with most main courses.

50 g (2½ oz) snow peas

50 g (2½ oz) kale, sliced

50 g (2½ oz) white cabbage, sliced

50 g (2½ oz) broccoli florets and stems, sliced

50 g (2½ oz) cauliflower florets

50 g (2½ oz) asparagus, cut into 2 inch lengths

50 g (2½ oz) Chinese or pak-choi cabbage, sliced

50 g (2½ oz) button mushrooms, halved

50 g (2½ oz) fresh baby corn, halved

150 ml (5 floz) chicken stock

½ tsp ground white pepper

75 ml (2½ floz) peanut or corn oil

3 tbsp finely chopped garlic

4 tbsp oyster sauce

1 tbsp white soy sauce

¼ tsp black soy sauce

ROASTED AUBERGINE SALAD

Yam Makheua Yao

SERVES 6

Dry-roast the aubergines in a 180°C/350°F/gas 4 oven for about 15–20 minutes until soft, then cool, remove the skin and slice into 1 inch pieces.

Sauté the pork in a frying pan or wok with a little oil over high heat until done, about 10 minutes. Mix the aubergine, pork, prawns and all the remaining ingredients together well in a bowl.

Serve accompanied by rice.

INGREDIENTS

3 long green aubergines, combined weight approx. 300 g (11 oz)
25 g (1 oz) ground pork
3 tbsp peanut or corn oil
50 g (2 oz) dried prawns, rinsed in hot water and drained
50 g (2 oz) shallots, sliced
5 fresh small green chillies, chopped roughly
2 tbsp lime juice
1 tsp fish sauce
¼ tsp sugar

Sticky Rice with Mangoes
Khao Niaow Ma Muang
SERVES 4 – 6

Ingredients

200 g (8 oz) sticky rice
1050 ml (35 floz) thin coconut milk
60 g (2½ oz) sugar
½ tsp salt
½ tsp cornflour
2 ripe mangoes, peeled and sliced

Soak the rice in water for 4 hours, rinse well 3 times in lukewarm water and drain very well. Line a strainer with cheesecloth, add the rice and place over a pan of boiling water—don't let the water touch the bottom of the rice.

Cover and steam for about 30 minutes until fairly soft.

Mix 900 ml (30 floz) of the coconut milk with the sugar and ¼ teaspoon of the salt. Stir in the rice and mix well.

Mix the remaining 150 ml (5 floz) of coconut milk with the ¼ teaspoon salt and the cornflour together in a small pan, bring to a boil, simmer for 2 minutes and cool.

Place the sticky rice onto serving plates, spoon the cornflour sauce over the top and arrange the mango slices around the edges.

STIR-FRIED GREENS
Phak Bung Fai Daeng

SERVES 4 – 6

INGREDIENTS

3 tbsp peanut or corn oil

300 g (11 oz) swamp cabbage leaves and stems, cut into 10cm lengths

150 ml (5 floz) chicken stock

2 tbsp marinated soya beans

1 tbsp chopped garlic

Heat the oil in a wok or pan until very hot. Add all the ingredients at once (watch for splattering), and stir-fry for about 2 minutes.

Serve accompanied by steamed rice.

INGREDIENTS

150 ml (5 floz) peanut or corn oil

200 g (7 oz) raw large shrimp, shelled

100 g (4 oz) firm tofu, diced

3 tbsp preserved sweet white radish, chopped

3 tbsp sliced shallots

4 eggs

300 g (11 oz) rice or cellophane noodles (sen lek or woon sen), soaked in cold water for 7–10 minutes, if dried

75 ml (2½ floz) chicken stock

3 tbsp dried prawns, chopped

30 g (1½ oz) unsalted peanuts, chopped

4 spring onions, sliced

400 g (15 oz) bean sprouts

Sauce

300 ml (10 floz)water

150 ml (5 floz) tamarind juice

60 g (2½ oz) palm sugar

1 tbsp white soy sauce

THAI-FRIED NOODLES
Kwitiaow Phad Thai
SERVES 6

Mix all the sauce ingredients together in a pan and boil until reduced to about 100 ml (2½ floz). Set aside to cool.

Heat the oil in a wok or pan until very hot, then add the prawns and bean curd and stir-fry lightly for 1 minute. Add the preserved radish and shallot, fry for 1 minute, and break in the eggs. Stir-fry for a minute, then add the noodles and chicken stock. When the noodles are soft (about 2 minutes), add the dried prawns, peanuts, spring onions and bean sprouts. Add the sauce, fry for a couple of minutes and serve.

Serve accompanied by chopped peanuts, chopped dry chillies, sugar, lime wedges, spring onions and fresh bean sprouts, all in small saucers.

BANANA COOKED IN COCONUT MILK
Gluai Buad Chii

SERVES 4

Slice the bananas lengthwise, then in half. Pour the coconut milk into a pan, add the sugar and salt. Bring to a boil, add the bananas, bring back to a boil for 2 minutes and then remove from the heat. Serve with the coconut milk.

Serve hot or cold.

INGREDIENTS

2–3 small, slightly green bananas

600 ml (20 floz) cups thin coconut milk

200 g (8 oz) sugar

¼ tsp salt

FRIED BANANAS
Gluai Tod

SERVES 4 – 6

INGREDIENTS

300 g (12 oz) rice flour

300 ml (5 floz) water

25 g (1 oz) unsweetened grated coconut

3 tbsp plain flour

3 tbsp sugar

2 tbsp sesame seeds

2 tsp baking powder

1 tsp salt

Approx. 1¾ l (3 pt) peanut or corn oil for deep-frying

450 g (1 lb) small, slightly green bananas, quartered

Mix together well in a bowl all the ingredients except the oil and bananas. Heat the oil in a wok or deep pan to about180°C/350°F/ gas 4.

Dip the banana pieces into the coconut batter and then deep-fry until brown but not dark, about 3 minutes. Turn over and cook for 2 more minutes. Take out with a slotted spoon and drain on kitchen paper.